π to 100000 Decimal Places

T Spivey

Contents

3.

1415926535897932384626433832795028841971693993751058209749445923078164062862089986280348253421170679821480865132823066470938446095505822317253594081284811174502841027019385211055596446229489549303819644288109756659334461284756482337867831652712019091456485669234603486104543266482133936072602491412737245870066063155881748815209209628292540917153643678925903600113305305488204665213841469519415116094330572703657595919530921861173819326117931051185480744623799627495673518857527248912279381830119491298336733624406566430860213949463952247371907021798609437027705392171762931767523846748184676694051320005681271452635608277857713427577896091736371787214684409012249534301465495585371050792279689258923542019956112129021960864034418159813629774771309960518707211349999998372978049951059731732816096318595024459455346908302642522308253344685035261931188171010003137838752886587533208381420617177669147303598253490428

75546873115956286388235378759375195778
18577805321712268066130019278766111959
09216420198938095257201065485863278865
93615338182796823030195203530185296899
57736225994138912497217752834791315155
74857242454150695950829533116861727855
88907509838175463746493931925506040092
77016711390098488240128583616035637076
60104710181942955596198946767837449448
25537977472684710404753464620804668425
90694912933136770289891521047521620569
66024058038150193511253382430035587640
24749647326391419927260426992279678235
47816360093417216412199245863150302861
82974555706749838505494588586926995690
92721079750930295532116534498720275596
02364806654991198818347977535663698074
26542527862551181841757467289097772793
80008164706001614524919217321721477235
01414419735685481613611573525521334757
41849468438523323907394143334547762416
86251898356948556209921922218427255025
42568876717904946016534668049886272327
91786085784838279679766814541009538830
78636095068006422512520511739298489608
41284886269456042419652850222106611863
06744278622039194945047123713786960956
36437191728746776465757396241389086583
26459958133904780275900994657640789512

69468398352595709825822620522489407726
71947826848260147699090264013639443745
53050682034962524517493996514314298091
90659250937221696461515709858387410597
88595977297549893016175392846813826868
38689427741559918559252459539594310499
72524680845987273644695848653836736222
62609912460805124388439045124413654976
27807977156914359977001296160894416948
68555848406353422072225828488648158456
02850601684273945226746767889525213852
25499546667278239864565961163548862305
77456498035593634568174324112515076069
47945109659609402522887971089314566913
68672287489405601015033086179286809208
74760917824938589009714909675985261365
54978189312978482168299894872265880485
75640142704775551323796414515237462343
64542858444795265867821051141354735739
52311342716610213596953623144295248493
71871101457654035902799344037420073105
78539062198387447808478489683321445713
86875194350643021845319104848100537061
46806749192781911979399520614196634287
54440643745123718192179998391015919561
81467514269123974894090718649423196156
79452080951465502252316038819301420937
62137855956638937787083039069792077346
72218256259966150142150306803844773454

3

92026054146659252014974428507325186660
02132434088190710486331734649651453905
79626856100550810665879699816357473638
40525714591028970641401109712062804390
39759515677157700420337869936007230558
76317635942187312514712053292819182618
61258673215791984148488291644706095752
70695722091756711672291098169091528017
35067127485832228718352093539657251210
83579151369882091444210067510334671103
14126711136990865851639831501970165151
16851714376576183515565088490998985998
23873455283316355076479185358932261854
89632132933089857064204675259070915481
41654985946163718027098199430992448895
75712828905923233260972997120844335732
65489382391193259746366730583604142813
88303203824903758985243744170291327656
18093773444030707469211201913020330380
19762110110044929321516084244485963766
98389522868478312355265821314495768572
62433441893039686426243410773226978028
07318915441101044682325271620105265227
21116603966655730925471105578537634668
20653109896526918620564769312570586356
62018558100729360659876486117910453348
85034611365768675324944166803962657978
77185560845529654126654085306143444318
58676975145661406800700237877659134401

71274947042056223053899456131407112700
04078547332699390814546646458807972708
26683063432858785698305235808933065757
40679545716377525420211495576158140025
01262285941302164715509792592309907965
47376125517656751357517829666454779174
50112996148903046399471329621073404375
18957359614589019389713111790429782856
47503203198691514028708085990480109412
14722131794764777262241425485454033215
71853061422881375850430633217518297986
62237172159160771669254748738986654949
45011465406284336639379003976926567214
63853067360965712091807638327166416274
88880078692560290228472104031721186082
04190004229661711963779213375751149595
01566049631862947265473642523081770367
51590673502350728354056704038674351362
22247715891504953098444893330963408780
76932599397805419341447377441842631298
60809988868741326047215695162396586457
30216315981931951673538129741677294786
72422924654366800980676928238280689964
00482435403701416314965897940924323789
69070697794223625082216889573837986230
01593776471651228935786015881617557829
73523344604281512627203734314653197777
41603199066554187639792933441952154134
18994854447345673831624993419131814809

2777710386387734317720754565453220770
9212019051660962804909263601975988216
1332316663652861932668633606273567603
5447762803504507772355471058595870279
0814356240145171806246436267945627531
8134078330336254232783944975382437058
3531147711992606381334677687969597309
8339130771098704085913374641442827726
3465947047458784778720192771528073767
9077071572134447306057007334924369113
8350493163128404251219256517980694135
2801314701304781643788518529092854201
1658393419656213491434159562586586570
5526904965209858033850722426482939785
8478316305777756068887644624824685792
0395352773480304802900587607582510474
0916439613626760449256274204208320856
1190625454337213153595845068772460290
6187667952406163425225771954291629919
0645537799140373404328752628889639958
9475729174642635745525407909145135711
3694109119393251910760208252026187985
1887705842972591677813149699009019211
9717372784768472686084900337702424291
5130050051683233643503895170298939223
4517220138128069650117844087451960121
2859937162313017114448464090389064495
4400619869075485160263275052983491874
7866808818338510228334508504860825039

02133219715518430635455007668282949304
13776552793975175461395398468339363830
47461199665385815384205685338621867252
33402830871123282789212507712629463229
56398989893582116745627010218356462201
34967151881909730381198004973407239610
36854066431939509790190699639552453005
45058068550195673022921913933918568034
49039820595510022635353619204199474553
85938102343955449597783779023742161727
11172364343543947822181852862408514006
66044332588856986705431547069657474585
50332323342107301545940516553790686627
33379958511562578432298827372319898757
14159578111963583300594087306812160287
64962867446047746491599505497374256269
01049037781986835938146574126804925648
79855614537234786733039046883834363465
53794986419270563872931748723320837601
12302991136793862708943879936201629515
41337142489283072201269014754668476535
76164773794675200490757155527819653621
32392640616013635815590742202020318727
76052772190055614842555187925303435139
844253222341576233610642506390497500865
62710953591946589751413103482276930624
74353632569160781547818115284366795706
11086153315044521274739245449454236828
86061340841486377670096120715124914043

7

02725386076482363414334623518975766452
16413767969031495019108575984423919862
91642193994907236234646844117394032659
18404437805133389452574239950829659122
85085558215725031071257012668302402929
52522011872676756220415420516184163484
75651699981161410100299607838690929160
30288400269104140792886215078424516709
08700069928212066041837180653556725253
25675328612910424877618258297651579598
47035622262934860034158722980534989650
22629174878820273420922224533985626476
69149055628425039127577102840279980663
65825488926488025456610172967026640765
59042909945681506526530537182941270336
93137851786090407086671149655834343476
93385781711386455873678123014587687126
60348913909562009939361031029161615288
13843790990423174733639480457593149314
05297634757481193567091101377517210080
31559024853090669203767192203322909433
46768514221447737939375170344366199104
03375111735471918550464490263655128162
28824462575916333039107225383742182140
88350865739177150968288747826569959957
44906617583441375223970968340800535598
49175417381883999446974867626551658276
58483588453142775687900290951702835297
16344562129640435231176006651012412006

59755851276178583829204197484423608007
19304576189323492292796501987518721272
67507981255470958904556357921221033346
69749923563025494780249011419521238281
53091140790738602515227429958180724716
25916685451333123948049470791191532673
43028244186041426363954800044800267049
62482017928964766975831832713142517029
69234889627668440323260927524960357996
46925650493681836090032380929345958897
06953653494060340216654437558900456328
82250545255640564482465151875471196218
44396582533754388569094113031509526179
37800297412076651479394259029896959469
95565761218656196733786236256125216320
86286922210327488921865436480229678070
57656151446320469279068212073883778142
33562823608963208068222468012248261177
18589638140918390367367222088832151375
56003727983940041529700287830766709444
74560134556417254370906979396122571429
89467154357846878861444581231459357198
49225284716050492212424701412147805734
55105000801908699603302763478708108175 4
50119307141223390866393833952942578690
50764310063835198343893415961318543475
46495569781038293097164651438407007073
60411237359984345225161050702705623526
60127648483084076118301305279320542746

9

28654036036745328651057065874882256981
57936789766974220575059683440869735020
14102067235850200724522563265134105592
40190274216248439140359989535394590944
07046912091409387001264560016237428802
10927645793106579229552498872758461012
64836999892256959688159205600101655256
37567856672279661988578279484885583439
75187445455129656344348039664205579829
36804352202770984294232533022576341807
03947699415979159453006975214829336655
56615678736400536665641654732170439035
21329543529169414599041608753201868379
37023488868947915107163785290234529244
07736594956305100742108714261349745956
15138498713757047101787957310422969066
67021449863746459528082436944578977233
00487647652413390759204340196340391147
32023380715095222010682563427471646024
33544005152126693249341967397704159568
37535551667302739007497297363549645332
88869844061196496162773449518273695588
22075735517665158985519098666539354948
10688732068599075407923424023009259007
01731960362254756478940647548346647760
41146323390565134330684495397907090302
34604614709616968868850140834704054607
42958699138296682468185710318879065287
03665083243197440477185567893482308943

10682870272280973624809399627060747264
55399253994428081137369433887294063079
26159599546262462970706259484556903471
19729964090894180595343932512362355081
34949004364278527138315912568989295196
42728757394691427253436694153236100453
73048819855170659412173524625895487301
67600298865925786628561249665523533829
42878542534048308330701653722856355915
25347844598183134112900199920598135220
51173365856407826484942764411376393866
92480311836445369858917544264739988228
46218449008777697763127957226726555625
96282542765318300134070922334365779160
12809317940171859859993384923549564005
70995585611349802524990669842330173503
58044081168552653117099570899427328709
25848789443646005041089226691783525870
78595129834417295351953788553457374260
85902908176515578039059464087350612322
61120093731080485485263572282576820341
60504846627750450031262008007998049254
85346941469775164932709504934639382432
22718851597405470214828971117779237612
25788734771881968254629812686858170507
40272550263329044976277894423621674119
18626943965067151577958675648239939176
04260176338704549901761436412046921823
70764887834196896861181558158736062938

60381017121585527266830082383404656475
88040513808016336388742163714064354955
61868964112282140753302655100424104896
78352858829024367090488711819090949453
31442182876618103100735477054981596807
72009474696134360928614849417850171807
79306810854690009445899527942439813921
35055864221964834915126390128038320010
97738680662877923971801461343244572640
09737425700735921003154150893679300816
99805365202760072774967458400283624053
46037263416554259027601834840306811381
85510597970566400750942608788573579603
73245141467867036880988060971642584975
95138069309449401515422221943291302173
91253835591503100330325111749156969 17
45027149433151558854039221640972291011
29035521815762823283182342548326111912
80092825256190205263016391147724733148
57391077758744253876117465786711694147
76421441111263583553871361011023267987
75641024682403226483464176636980663785
76813492045302240819727856471983963087
81543221166912246415911776732253264335
68614618654522268126887268445968442416
10785401676814208088502800541436131462
30821025941737562389942075713627516745
73189189456283525704413354375857534269
86994725470316566139919996826282472706

41336222178923903176085428943733935618
89165125042440400895271983787386480584
72689546243882343751788520143956005710
48119498842390606136957342315590796703
46149143447886360410318235073650277859
08975782727313050488939890099239135033
73250855982655867089242612429473670193
90772713070686917092646254842324074855
03660801360466895118400936686095463250
02145852930950000907151058236267293264
53738210493872499669933942468551648326
11341461106802674466373343753407642940
26682973865220935701626384648528514903
62932019919968828517183953669134522244
47080459239660281715655156566611135982
31122506289058549145097157553900243931
53519090210711945730024388017661503527
08626025378817975194780610137150044899
17210022201335013106016391541589578037
11779277522597874289191791552241718958
53616805947412341933984202187456492564
43462392531953135103311476394911995072
85843065836193536932969928983791494193
94060857248639688369032655643642166442
57607914710869984315733749648835292769
32822076294728238153740996154559879825
98910937171262182830258481123890119682
21429457667580718653806506487026133892
82299497257453033283896381843944770779

13

4022843598834100358385423897354243 9564
7555684095224844554139239410001 6207693
6368467764130178196593799715574 6854194
6334893748439129742391433659360 4100352
3437770658886778113949861647874 7140793
2638587386247328896456435987746 6763847
9466504074111825658378878454858 1489629
6127399841344272608606187245545 2360643
1537101127468097787044640947582 8034876
9758948328241239292960582948619 1966709
1895808983320121031843034012849 5116203
5342801441276172858302435598300 3204202
4512072872535581195840149180969 2533950
7577840006746552603144616705082 7682772
2235341911026341631571474061238 5042584
5988419907611287258059113935689 6014316
6828317632356732541707342081733 2230462
9879928049085140947903688786878 9493054
6955703072619009502076433493359 1060245
4508645362893545686295853131533 7183868
2656178622736371697577418302398 6006591
4816164049449650117321313895747 0620884
7480236537103115089842799275442 6853277
9743113951435741722197597993596 8525228
5745263796289612691572357986620 5734083
7576687388426640599099350500081 3375432
4546359675048442352848747014435 4541957
6258473564216198134073468541117 6688311
8654489377697956651727966232671 4810338

64391375186594673002443450054499539974
23723287124948347060440634716063258306
49829795510109541836235030309453097335
83446283947630477564501500850757894954
89313939448992161255255977014368589435
85877526379625597081677643800125436502
37141278346792610199558522471722017772
37004178084194239487254068015560359983
90548985723546745642390585850216719031
39526294455439131663134530893906204678
43877850542393905247313620129476918749
75191011472315289326772533918146607300
08902776896311481090220972452075916729
70078505807171863810549679731001678708
50694207092232908070383263453452038027
86099055690013413718236837099194951648
96007550493412678764367463849020639640
19766685592335654639138363185745698147
19621084108096188460545603903845534372
91414465134749407848844237721751543342
60306698831768331001133108690421939031
08014378433415137092435301367763108491
35161564226984750743032971674696406665
31527035325467112667522460551199581831
96376370761799191920357958200759560530
23462677579439363074630569010801149427
14100939136913810725813781357894005599
50018354251184172136055727522103526803
73572652792241737360575112788721819084

49006178013889710770822931002797665935
83875890939568814856026322439372656247
27760378908144588378550197028437793624
07825052704875816470324581290878395232
45323789602984166922548964971560698119
21865849267704039564812781021799132174
16305810554598801300484562997651121241
53637451500563507012781592671424134210
33015661653560247338078430286552572227
53049998837015348793008062601809623815
16136690334111386538510919367393835522
93458883225508870645075394739520439680
79067086806445096986548801682874343786
12645381583428075306184548590379821799
45996811544197425363443996029025100158
88272164745006820704193761584547123183
46007262933955054823955713725684023226
82130124767945226448209102356477527230
82081063518899152692889108455571126603
96503439789627825001611015323516051965
59042118449499077899920073294769058685
77878720982901352956613978884860509786
08595701773129815531495168146717695976
09942100361835591387778176984587581044
66283998806006162298486169353373865787
73598336161338413385368421197893890018
52956919678045544828584837011709672125
35338758621582310133103877668272115726
94951817958975469399264219791552338576

62316762754757035469941489290413018638
61194391962838870543677743224276809132
36544948536676800000106526248547305586
15989991401707698385483188750142938908
99506854530765116803337322265175662207
52695179144225280816517166776672793035
48515420402381746089232839170327542575
08676551178593950027933895920576682789
67764453184040418554010435134838953120
13263783692835808271937831265496174599
70567450718332065034556644034490453627
56001125018433560736122276594927839370
64784264567633881880756561216896050416
11390390639601620221536849410926053876
88714837989559999112099164646441191856
82770045742434340216722764455893301277
81586869525069499364610175685060167145
35431581480105458860564550133203758645
48584032402987170934809105562116715468
48477803944756979804263180991756422809
87399876697323769573701580806822904599
21236616890259627304306793165311494017
64737693873514093361833216142802149763
39918983548487562529875242387307755955
59554651963944018218409984124898262367
37714672260616336432964063357281070788
75816404381485018841143188598827694490
11932129682715888413386943468285900666
40806314077757725705630729400492940302

17

4204984165654797367054855804458657202276378404668233798528271057843197535417
9501134727362577408021347682604502285157979579764746702284099956160156910890
3845824502679265942055503958792298185264800706837650418365620945554346135134
1525700659748819163413595567196496540321872716026485930490397874895890661272
5079482827693895352175362185079629778514618843271922322381015874445052866523
8022532843891375273845892384422535472653098171578447834215822327020690287232
3300538621634798850946954720047952311201504329322662827276321779088400878614
8022147537657810581970222630971749507212724847947816957296142365859578209083
0733233560348465318730293026659645013718375428897557971449924654038681799213
8934692447419850973346267933210726868707680626399193619650440995421676278409
1466985692571507431574079380532392523947755744159184582156251819215523370960
7483329234921034514626437449805596103307994145347784574699992128599999399612
2816152193148887693880222810830019860165494165426169685867883726095877456761
8250727599295089318052187292461086763995891614585505839727420980909781729323
9301067663868240401113040247007350857

18

28724627134946368531815469690466968693
92547251941399291465242385776255004748
52954768147954670070503479995888676950
16124972282040303995463278830695976249
36151010243655535223069061294938859901
57346610237122354789112925476961760050
47974928060721268039226911027772261025
44149221576504508120677173571202718024
29681062037765788371669091094180744878
14049075517820385653909910477594141321
54328440625030180275716965082096427348
41469572639788425600845312140659358090
41271135920041975985136254796160632288
73618136737324450607924411763997597461
93835845749159880976744709300654 63424
23460634237474666080431701260052055928
49369594143408146852981505394717890045
18357551541252235905906872648786357525
41911288877371766374860276606349603536
79470269232297186832771739323619200777
45221262475186983349515101986426988784
71719396649769070825217423365662725928
44062043021411371992278526998469884770
23238238400556555178890876613601304770
98438611687052310553149162517283732728
67600724817298763756981633541507460883
86636406934704372066886512756882661497
30788657015685016918647488541679154596
50723428773069985371390430026653078398

19

77638503238182155355973235306860430106
75760838908627049841888595138091030423
59578249514398859011318583584066747237
02971497850841458530857813391562707603
56390763947311455495832266945702494139
83163433237897595568085683629725386791
32750555425244919435891284050452269538
12179131914513500993846311774017971512
28378546011603595540286440590249646693
07077690554810288502080858008781157738
17191741776017330738554758006056014337
74329901272867725304318251975791679296
99650414607066457125888346979796429316
22965520168797300035646304579308840327
48077181155533090988702550520768046303
46086581653948769519600440848206596737
94731680864156456505300498816164905788
31154345485052660069823093157776500378
07046612647060214575057932709620478256
15247145918965223608396645624105195510
52235723973951288181640597859142791481
65426328920042816091369377737222999833
27082082969955737727375667615527113922
58805520189887620114168005468736558063
34716037342917039079863965229613128017
82679717289822936070288069087768660593
25274637840539769184808204102194471971
38692560841624511239806201131845412447
82050110798760717155683154078865439041

```
21087303240201068534194723047666672174
98698685470767812051247367924791931508
56444775379853799732234456122785843296
84664751333657369238720146472367942787
00425032555899268843495928761240075587
56946413705625140011797133166207153715
43600687647731867558714878398908107429
53094106059694431584775397009439883949
14432353668539209946879645066533985738
88786614762944341401049888993160051207
67810358861166020296119363968213496075
01116498327856353161451684576956871090
02999769841263266502347716728657378579
08574664607722834154031144152941880478
25438761770790430001566986776795760909
96693607559496515273634981189641304331
16627747123388174060373174397054067031
09676765748695358789670031925866259410
51053358438465602339179674926784476370
84749783336555790073841914731988627135
25954625181604342253729962863267496824
05806029642114638643686422472488728343
41704415734824818333016405669596688667
69563491416328426414974533349999480002
66998758881593507357815195889900539512
08535103572613736403436753471410483601
75464883004078464167452167371904831096
76711344349481926268111073994825060739
49507350316901973185211955263563258433
```

21

90998224986240670310768318446607291248
74754031617969941139738776589986855417
03188477886759290260700432126661791922
35209382278788809886335991160819235355
57046463491132085918979613279131975649
09760001399623444553501434642686046449
58624769094347048293294140411146540923
98834443515913320107739441118407410768
49810663472410482393582740194493566516
10884631256785297769734684303061462418
03585293315973458303845541033701091676
77637427621021370135485445092630719011
47318485749233181672072137279355679528
44392548156091372812840633303937356242
00160456645574145881660521666087387480
47243391212955877763906969037078828527
75389405246075849623157436917113176134
78388271941686066257210368513215664780
01476752310393578606896111259960281839
30954870905907386135191459181951029732
78755710497290114871718971800469616977
70017913919613791417162707018958469214
34369676292745910994006008498356842520
19155937037010110497473394938778859894
17433031785348707603221982970579751191
44051099423588303454635349234982688362
40433272674155403016195056806541809394
09982020609994140216890900708213307230
89662119775530665918814119157783627292

22

74615618571037217247100952142369648308
64102592887457999322374955191221951903
42445230753513380685680735446499512720
31744871954039761073080602699062580760
20292731455252078079914184290638844373
49968145827337207266391767020118300464
81900024130835088465841521489912761065
13741539435657211390328574918769094413
70209051703148777346165287984823533829
72601361109845148418238081205409961252
74580881099486972216128524897425555516
07637167505489617301680961380381191436
11439921063800508321409876045993093248
51025168294467260666138151745712559754
95358023998314698220361338082849935670
55755247129027453977621404931820146580
08021566536067765508783804304134310591
80460680083459113664083488740800574127
25867047922583191274157390809143831384
56424150940849133918096840251163991936
85322555733896695374902662092326131885
58915808324555719484538756287861288590
04106006073746501402627824027346962528
21717494158233174923968353013617865367
37606421667781377399510065895288774276
62636841830680190804609849809469763667
33566228291513235278880615776827815958
86691802389403330764419124034120223163
68577860357276941541778826435238131905

02808701857504704631293335375728538660
58889045831114507739429352019943219711
71642235005644042979892081594307167019
85746927384865383343614579463417592257
38985880016980147574205429958012429581
05456510831046297282937584161162532562
51657249807849209989799062003593650993
47215829651741357984910471116607915874
36986541222348341887722929446335178653
85673196255985202607294767407261676714
55736498121056777168934849176607717052
77187601199908144113058645577910525684
30481144026193840232247093924980293355
07318458903553971330884461741079591625
11714864874468611247605428673436709046
67846867027409188101424971114965781772
42793470702166882956108777944050484375
28443375108828264771978540006509704033
02186255614733211777117441335028160884
03517814525419643203095760186946490886
81545285621346988355444560249556668436
60292219512483091060537720198021831010
32704178386654471812603971906884623708
57518080035327047185659499476124248110
99928867915896904956394762460842406593
09486215076903149870206735338483495508
36366017848771060809804269247132410009
46401437360326564518456679245666955100
15022983307984960799498824970617236744

24

93612262229617908143114146609412341593
59309585407913908720832273354957208075
71651718765994498569379562387555161757
54380917805280294642004472153962807463
60211329425591600257073562812638733106
00589106524570802447493754318414940148
21199962764531068006631183823761639663
18093144467129861552759820145141027560
06892975024630401735148919457636078935
28555053173314164570504996443890936308
43874484783961684051845273288403234520
24705685164657164771393237755172947951
26132398229602394548579754586517458787
71331813875295980941217422730035229650
80891777050682592488223221549380483714
54781647213976820963320508305647920482
08592047549985732038887639160199524091
89389455767687497308569559580106595265
03036266159750662225084067428898265907
51063756356996821151094966974458054728
86936310203678232501823237084597901115
48472087618212477813266330412076216587
31297081123075815982124863980721240786
88781145016558251361789030708608701989
75889807456643955157415363193191981070
57533663373803827152798849350397480001
58905194208797113080512339332219034662
49917169150948541401871060354603794643
37900589095772118080446574396280618671

78610171567409676620802957665770512912
09907944304632892947306159510430902221
43937184956063405618934251305726829146
57832933405246350289291754708725648426
00349629611654138230077313327298305001
60256724014185152041890701154288579920
81219844931569990591820118197335001261
87728036812481995877070207532406361259
31343859554254778196114293516356122349
66615226147353996740515849986035529533
29245752388810136202347624669055816438
96786309762736550472434864307121849437
34853006063876445662721866617012381277
15621379746149861328744117714552444708
99714452288566294244023018479120547849
85745216346964489738920624019435183100
88283480249249085403077863875165911302
87395878709810077271827187452901397283
66148421428717055317965430765045343246
00536361472618180969976933486264077435
19992868632383508875668359509726557481
54319401955768504372480010204137498318
72259677387154958399718444907279141965
84593008394263702087563539821696205532
48032122674989114026785285996734052420
31091797899905718821949391320753431707
98002373659098537552023891164346718558
29068537118979526262344924833924963424
49714656846591248918556629589329909035

23923333364743520370770101084388003290
75983421701855422838616172104176030116
45918780539367447472059985023582891833
69292233732399948043710841965947316265
48257480994825099918330069765693671596
89364493348864744213500840700660883597
23503953234017958255703601693699098867
11321097988970705172807558551912699306
73099250704070245568507786790694766126
29808225163313639952117098452809263037
59224267425755998928927837047444521893
63203489415521044597261883800300677617
93138139916205806270165102445886924764
92468919246121253102757313908404700071
43561362316992371694848132554200914530
41037135453296620639210547982439212517
25401323149027405858920632175894943454
89068463993137570910346332714153162232
80552297297953801880162859073572955416
27886764982741861642187898857410716490
69191851162815285486794173638906653885
76422915834250067361245384916067413734
01735727799563410433268835695078149313
78007362354180070619180267328551191942
67609122103598746924117283749312616339
50012395992405084543756985079570462226
64619000103500490183034153545842833764
37811198855631877779253720116671853954
18359844383052037628194407615941068207

27

169703022851522505731260930468984234333
152732131361216582808075212631547730600
442377475350595228717440266638914881710
730864361113890694202790881431194487990
417154042103412190847094080254023932940
294549387864023051292711909751353600090
219711054120966831115163287054230284700
073120658032626417116165957613272351560
666253667271899853419989523688483099930
027574199164638414270779887088742292770
053891227172486322028898425125287217820
603050099451082478357290569198855546780
860794628053712270424665431921452817600
741482403827835829719301017888345674160
781139895475044833931468963076339665720
267270433932167454218245570625247972190
978668542798977992339579057581890622520
547358220523642485078340711014498047870
266919901864388229323053823185597328690
780922253529591017341407334884761005560
401824239219269506208318381454698392360
646136398910121021770959767049083050810
854704194664371312299692358895384930130
635657618610606222870559942337163102120
784574464639897381885667462608794820180
647487672727222062676465338099801966880
368099415907577685263986514625333631240
505364026105696055131838131742611844200
189088853196356986962795036738424313010

13317533053298020166888174813429886815
85577810343231753064784983210629718425
18438553442762012823457071698853051832
61796411785796088881503296022907056144
76220915094739035946646916235396809201
39457817589108893199211226007392814916
94816152738427362642980982340632002440
24495894456129167049508235812487391799
64864113348032475777521970893277226234
94860150466526814398770516153170266969
29704928316285504212898146706195331970
26950721437823047687528028735412616639
17082459251700107141808548006369232594
62019002278087409859771921805158532147
39265325155903541020928466592529991435
37918253145452905984158176370589279069
09896911164381187809435371521332261443
62531449012745477269573939348154691631
16249288735747188240715039950094467319
54316193855485207665738825139639163576
72315100555603726339486720820780865373
49424401157996675073607111593513319591
97120948964717553024531364770942094635
69698222667377520994516845064362382421
18535348879893956731878066061078854400
05508276570305587448541805778891719207
88142335113866292966717964346876007704
79995378833878703487180218424373421122
73940255717690819603092018240188427057

0460926225641783752652633583242406125
3311529423457965569502506810018310900 4
1124537901533296615697052237921032570 6
9370510908307894799990049993953221536 2
2748476603613677697978567386584670936 6
7958858378879562594646489137665219958 8
2869338018360119323685785585581955560 4
2156250883650203322024513762158204618 1
0670519533065306060650105488716724537 7
9428313388716313955969058320834168984 7
6065607118347136218123246227258841990 2
8614208728495687963932546428534307530 1
1052857138296437099903569488852851904 0
2956047346131138263878897551788560424 9
9874831638280404684861893818959054203 9
8898726506976202019955484126500053944 2
8203930127481638158530396439925470201 6
7275932857436661644110962566337305409
2195196751483287348089574777752783442 2
1091073111351828046036347198185655572 9
5714474768255285786334934285842311874 9
4400032296906977583159038580393535213 5
8860079600342097547392296733310649395 6
0181223781285458431760556173386112673 4
7807458506760630482294096530411183066 7
1081893031108871728167519579675347188 5
3722930961614320400638132246584111115 7
7583585811350185690478153689381377184 7
2814751998350504781297718599084707621 9

74605887423256995828892535041937958260
61621184236876851141831606831586799460
16520577405294230536017803133572632670
54790338401257305912339601880137825421
92709476733719198728738524805742124892
11834708766296672072723256505651293331
26059505777727542471241648312832982072
36175057467387012820957554430596839555
56868611883971355220844528526400812520
27665557677495969626612604565245684086
13923826576858338469849977872670655519
18544686984694784957346226062942196245
57085371272776523098955450193037732166
64918257815467729200521266714346320963
78918523232150189761260343736840671941
93037746880999296877582441047878123266
25318184596045385354383911449677531286
42609252115376732588667226040425234910
87026958099647595805794663973419064010
03636190404203311357933654242630356145
70090112448008900208014780566037101541
22328891465722393145076071670643556827
43774396578906797268743847307634645167
75621030986040927170909512808630902973
85044527182892749689212106670081648583
39553773591913695015316201890888748421
07987068991148046692706509407620465027
72528650728905328548561433160812693005
69378541786109696920253886503457718317

66868859236814884752764984688219497397
29707737187188400414323127636504814531
12285099002074240925585925292610302106
73681543470152523487863516439762358604
19194129697690405264832347009911154242
60127343802208933109668636789869497799
40012601642276092608234930411806438291
38347354679725399262338791582998486459
27173405922562074910530853153718291168
16372193951887009577881815868504645076
99343940987433514431626330317247747486
89791820923948083314397084067308407958
93581089665647758599055637695252326536
14424780230826811831037735887089240613
03133647737101162821461466167940409051
86152603600925219472188909181073358719
64142144478654899528582343947050079830
38853886083103571930600277119455802191
19428999227223534587075662469261776631
78855144350218287026685610665003531050
21631820601760921798468493686316129372
79518730789726373537171502563787335797
71808184878458866504335824377004147710
41493492743845758710715973155943942641
25702709651251081155482479394035976811
88117282472158250109496096625393395380
92219559191818855267806214992317276316
32183398969380756168559117529984501320
67129392404144593862398809381240452191

48483164621014738918251010909677386906
64041589736104764365000680771056567184
86281496371118832192445663945814491486
16550049567698269030891118568798692947
05135248160917432430153836847072928989
82846022237301452655679898627767968091
46979837826876431159883210904371561129
97665215396354644208691975673700057387
64978437686287681792497469438427465256
31632300555130417422734164645512781278
45777724575203865437542828256714128858
34544435132562054464241011037955464190
58116862305964476958705407214198521210
67343324107567675758184569906930460475
22770167005684543969234041711089888993
41635058515788735343081552081177207188
03791040469830695786854739376564336319
79786803671873079693924236321448450354
77631567025539006542311792015346497792
90662415083288583952905426376876689688
05033172278001858850697362324038947000
47189761934734430843744375992503417880
79722358591342458131440498477017323616
94719765715353197754997162785663119046
91260918259124989036765417697990362375
52865263757337635269693443544004730671
98868901968147428767790866979688522501
63694985673021752313252926537589641517
14795595387842784998664563028788319620

33

99830494519874396369070682762657485810
43911223261879405994155406327013198989
57037611053236062986748037791537675115
83043208498720920280929752649812569163
42500052290887264692528466610466539217
14820801305022980526378364269597337070
53922789153510568883938113249757071331
02950443034671598944878684711643832805
06925077662745001220035262037094660234
14648998390252588830148678162196775194
58316771876275720050543979441245990077
11520515461993050983869825428464072555
40927403132571632640792934183342147090
41254253352324802193227707535554679587
16383587501815933871742360615511710131
23525633485820365146141870049205704372
01826173319471570086757853933607862273
95581857975872587441025420771054753612
94047460100094095444959662881486915903
89907186598056361713769222729076419775
51777201042764969496110562205925024202
17704269622154958726453989227697660310
52498085575947163107587013320886146326
64125911486338812202844406941694882615
29577625325019870359870674380469821942
05638125583343642194923227593722128905
64209430823525440841108645453694049692
71494003319782861318186188811118408257
86592875742638445005994422956858646048

10330153889114994869354360302218109434
66764000022362550573631294626296096198
76056425996394613869233083719626595473
92346241345977957485246478379807956931
98650815977675350553918991151335252298
73611277918274854200868953965835942196
33315028695611920122988898870060799927
95411188269023078913107603617634779489
43203210277335941690865007193280401716
38406449878717537567811853213284082165
71107549528294974936214608215583205687
23218557406516109627487437509809223021
16099826330339154694946444910045152809
25089745074896760324090768983652940657
92019831526541065813682379198409064571
24689484702093577611931399802468134052
00394781949866202624008902150166163813
53838151503773502296607462795291038406
86855690701575166241929872444827194293
31004854824454580718897633003232525821
58128032746796200281476243182862217105
43528983482082734516801861317195933247
11074662228508710666117703465352839577
62599774467218571581612641114327179434
78859908928084866949141390977167369002
77758502686646540565950394867841110790
11610400857274456293842549416759460548
71172359464291058509099502149587931121
96135908315882620682332156153086833730

83817327932819698387508708348388046388
47844188400318471269745437093732983624
02875197920802321878744882872843727378
01782700805878241074935751488997891173
97461293203510814327032514090304874622
62942344327571260086642508333187688650
75642927160552528954492153765175149219
63671810494353178583834538652556566406
57251363575064353236508936790431702597
87817719031486796384082881020946149007
97151377170990619549696400708676671023
30048672631475510537231757114322317411
41168062286420638890621019235522354671
16621374996932693217370431059872250394
56574924616978260970253359475020913836
67377289443869640002811034402608471289
90007468077648440887113413525033678773
16797709372778682166117865344231732264
63784769787514433209534000165069213054
64768909850502030150448808342618452087
30530973189492916425322933612431514306
57826407028389840984160295030924189712
09716016492656134134334222988279099217
86042679812457285345801338260995877178
11310216734025656274400729683406619848
06766158050216918337236803990279316064
20436812079900316264449146190219458229
69099212278855394878353830564686488165
55622943156731282743908264506116289428

36

03501661336697824051770155219626522725
45585073864058529983037918035043287670
38092521679075712040612375963276856748
45079151147313440001832570344920909712
43580944790046249431345502890068064870
42935340374360326258205357901183956490
89354345101342969617545249573960621490
28872893279252069653538639644322538832
75224996059869747598823299162635459733
24445163755334377492928990581175786355
55556269374269109471170021654117182195
05198317871371060510637955585889055688
52887989084750915764639074693619881507
81468526213325247383765119299015610918
97779220087057933964638274906806987691
68197492365624226087154176100430608904
37797667851966189140414492527048088197
14988015420577870065215940092897776013
30756847966992955433656139847738060394
36889588764605498387147896848280538470
17308711177611596635050399793438693391
19789887109156541709133082607647406305
71141109883938809548143782847452883836
80794188843426662220704387228874139478
01017721392281911992365405516395893474
26395382482960903690028835932774585506
08013179884071624465639979482757836501
95514221551339281978226984278638391679
71509126241054872570092407004548848569

37

2950448110738087996547481568913935380943474556972128919827177020766613602489581468119133614121258783895577357194986317210844398901423948496659251731388171602663261931065366535041473070804414939169363262373767770958503132559900957627319573086480424677012123270205337426670531424482081681303063973787366424836725398374876909806021827857862165127385635132901489035098832706172589325753639939790557291751600976154590447716922658063151110280384360173747421524760851520990161585823125715907334217365762671423904782795872815050956330928026684589376496497702329736413190609827406335310897924642421345837409011169391964250459128813403498810635400887596820054408364386516617880557608956896727531538081942077332597917278437625661184319891025007491829086475149794003160703845549465385946027452447466812314687943441610993338908992638411847425257044572517459325738989565185716575961481266020310797628254165590506042479114016957900338356574869252800743025623419498286467914476322774005529460903940177536335655471931000175430047504719144899841040015867946179241610016454716551337074073950260442769538553834397550548871

09978520540117516974758134492607943368
95437832211724506873442319898788441285
42064742809735625807066983106979935260
69339213568588139121480735472846322778
49080870024677763036055512323866562951
78853719673034634701222939581606792509
15321748903084088651606111901149844341
23501246469280288059961342835118847154
49771278473361766285062169778717743824
36256571177945006447771837022199910669
50216567576440449979407650379999548450
02710665987813603802314126836905783190
46079276529727769404361302305178708054
65115424693952651271010529270703066730
24447125973939950514628404767431363739
97825918454117641332790640063658415292
70190302760173394748669603486949765417
52429306040727005090395031485229213 92
57559484507886797792525393176515641619
71684435243697944473559642606333910551
26826061595726217036698506473281266724
52198906054988028078288142979633669674
41248059821921463395657457221022986775
99746738126069367069134081559412016115
96019023775352555630060624798326124988
12881929373434768626892192397778339107
33106588256813777172328315329082525092
73304785072497713944833389255208117560
84529665905539409655685417060011798572

39

93813998258319293679100391844099286575
60599359891000296986446097471471847010
15312837626311467742091455740418159088
00064943237855839308530828305476076799
52435739163122188605754967383224319565
06554608528812019023636447127037486344
21727257879503428486312944916318475347
53143504139209610879605773098720135248
40750576371992536504709085825139368634
63863368042891767107602111159828875539
94012007601394703366179371539630613986
36554922137415979051190835882900976566
47300733879314678913181465109316761575
82135142486044229244530411316065270097
43300884990346754055186406773426035834
09608605533747362760935658853109760994
23834738222208729246449768456057956251
67655740884103217313456277358560523582
36389532038534024842273371639123973215
99544082842166663602329654569470357718
48734420342277066538738750061692127680
15766181095420097708363604361110592409
11788954033802142652394892968643980892
61146354145715351943428507213534530183
15875628275733898268898523557799295727
64522939156747756667605108788764845349
36360682780505646228135988858792599409
46446041705204470046315137975431737187
75603981596264750141090665886616218003

82669899619655805872086397211769952194
66789857011798332440601811575658074284
18291061519391763005919431443460515404
77105700543390001824531177337189558576
03607182860506356479979004139761808955
36366960316219311325022385179167205518
06592635180362512145759262383693482226
65895576994660491938112486609099798128
57182349400661555219611220720309227764
62009993152442735894887105766238946938
89446495093960330454340842102462401048
72332875008174917987554387938738143989
42380117627008371960530943839400637561
16458560943129517597713935396074322792
48922126704580818331376416581826956210
58728924477400359470092686626596514220
50630078592002488291860839743732353849
08396432614700053242354064704208949921
02504047267810590836440074663800208701
26664209457181702946752278540074508552
37772089058168391844659282941701828823
30149715542352359117748186285929676050
48203864343108779562892925405638946621
94826871104282816389397571175778691543
01650586029652174595819888786804081103
28432739867198621306205559855266036405
04628215230615459447448990883908199973
87474529698107762014871340001225355222
46695409315213115337915798026979555710

41

50850747387475075806876537644578252443
26380461430428892359348529610582693821
03498000405248407084403561167817170512
81337880570564345061611933042444079826
03779511985486945591520519600930412710
07277849301555038895360338261929343797
08187432094991415959339636811062755729
52780042548630600545238391510689989135
78820019411786535682149118528207852130
12551851849371150342215954224451190020
73935339627400208110465530207932867 2547
40543652717595893500716336076321614725
81540764205302004534018357233829266191
53083540951202263291650544261236191970
51613839357326693760156914429944943744
85680977569630312958871916112929468188
49363386473927476012269641588489009657
17086160598147204467428664208765334799
85822209061980217321161423041947775499
07387385679411898246609130916917722742
07233367635032678340586301930193242996
39720444517928812285447821195353089891
01253429755247276357302262813820918074
39748671453590778633530160821559911314
14420509144729353502223081719366350934
68658586563148555758624478186201087118
89760652969899269328178705576435143382
06014107732926106343152533718224338526
35202177354407152818981376987551575745

42

46939727150488469793619500477720970561
79391382898984532742622728864710888327
01737232588182446584362495805925603381
05215606206155713299156084892064340303
39526226345145428367869828807425142256
74518061841495646861116354049718976821
54227722479474033571527436819409892050
11365340012384671429655186734415374161
50425632567134302476551252192180357801
69240326699541746087592409207004669340
39651017813485783569444076047023254075
55577647284507518268904182939661133101
60131119077398632462778219023650660374
04160672496249013743321724645409741299
55705291424382080760983648234659738866
91349919784013108015581343979194852830
43673901248208244481412809544377389832
00598649091595053228579145768849625786
65885999179867520554558099004556461178
75524937012455321717019428288461740273
66499784755082942280202329012216301023
09772151569446427909802190826689868834
26307160920791408519769523555348865774
34252775311972474308730436195113961190
80030255878387644206085044730631299277
88894272918972716989057592524467966018
97074829609491906487646937027507738664
32391919042254290235318923377293166736
08699622803255718530891928440380507103

0064776847863243191000223929297852553723
75566213644740096760539439838235764606
99246526008909062410590421545392790441
15295803453345002562441010063595300395
98864466169595626351878060688513723462
70799732723313469397145628554261546765
06324656766202792452085813477176085216
91340946520307673391841147504140168924
12131982688156866456148538028753933116
02322925556189410429953356400957864953
40935115266454024418775949316930560448
68642086275720117231952640502309977456
76478384889734643172159806267876718380
05247696884084989185086149003432403476
74268624595239589035858213500645099817
82446360873177543788596776729195261112
13859194725451400301180503437875277664
40276261894101757687268042817662386068
04778852428874302591452470739505465251
35339459598789619778911041890292943818
56720507096460626354173294464957661265
19534957018600154126239622864138977967
33329070567376962156498184506842263690
3678495559700260798679926101903933126
37685569687670292953711625280055431007
86408728939225714512481135778627664902
42516199027747109033593330930494838059
78566288447874414698414990671237647895
82263294904679812089984857163571087831

19184863025450162092980582920833481363
84054217200561219893536693713367333924
64416125223196943471206417375491216357
00857369439730597970971972666664226743
11177621764030686813103518991122713397
24036887000996862922546465006385288620
39380050477827691283560337254825579391
29852515068299691077542576474883253414
12132800626717094009098223529657957997
80301828242849022147074811112401860761
34151503875698309186527806588966823625
23937845272634530420418802508442363190
38331838455052236799235775292910692504
32614469501098610888999146585518818735
82528164302520939285258077969737620845
63748211443398816271003170315133440230
95263519295886806908213558536801610002
13740851154484912685841268695899174149
13382057849280069825519574020181810564
12972508360703568510553317878408290000
41552511865779453963317538532092149720
52660783126028196116485809868458752512
99974040927976831766399146553861089375
87952214971731728131517932904431121815
87102351874075722210012376872194474720
93493123241070650806185623725267325407
33324875754482967573450019321902199119
96079798937338367324257610393898534927
87774739805080800155447640610535222023

45

25409443567718794565430406735896491017
61077594836454082348613025471847648518
95758366743997915085128580206078205544
62991723202028222914886959399729974297
47115537185892423849385585859540743810
48826246487880533042714630119415898963
28792678327322456103852197011130466587
10050008328517731177648973523092666123
45888731028835156264460236719966445547
27608310118788389151149340939344750073
02585581475619088139875235781233134227
98665035227253671712307568610450045489
70360079569827626392344107146584895780
24140815840522953693749971066559489445
92462866199635563506526234053394391421
11271810691052290024657423604130093691
88925586578466846121567955425660541600
50712766417660568742742003295771606434
48606201239821698271723197826816628249
93871499544913730205184366907672357740
00539326626227603236597517189259018011
04290384274185507894887438832703063283
27996300720069801244365116394086922222
07453202446241211558043545420642151215
85056896157356414313068883443185280853
97592773443365538418834030351782294625
37020157821573732655231857635540989540
33236382319219892171177449469403678296
18592080340386757583411151882417743914

50773663840718804893582568685420116450
31357633355509440319236720348651010561
04987272647213198654343545040913185951
31451812764373104389725070049819870521
76272494065214619959232142314439776546
70835171474936798618655279171582408065
10637995001842959387991583501715807598
83784962257398512129810326379376218322
45659423668537679911314010804313973233
54490908249104991433258432988210339846
98141715756010829706583065211347076803
68069532297199059990445120908727577622
53510409023928877942463048328031913127
10495478599180196967835321464441189260
63152661816744319355081708187547705080
26540252941092182648582138575266881555
84113198560022135158887210365696087515
06318753300294211868222189377554602722
72912905042922597877106678738400006167
72154638441292371193521828499824350920
89180168557279815642185819119749098573
05703326676464607287574305653726027689
82373259745084479649545648030771598153
95582777913937360171742299602735310276
87194494449179397851446315973144353518
50491413941557329382048542123508173912
54974981930871439661513294204591938010
62314217741991840601803479498876910515
57905554806953878540066453375981862846

47

41990522045280330626369562649091082762
71159038569950512465299960628554438383
30327638599800792922846659503551211245
28408751622906026201185777531374794936
20554964010730013488531507354873539056
02908933526400713274732621960311773433
94367338575912450814933573691166454128
17881714540230547506671365182582848980
99512139193995633241336556777098003081
91027204099714868741813466700609405102
14626902804491596465453301077546954130
88714165312544813061192407821188690056
02778182423502269618934435254763357353
64856193632544177566139817039306328721
66905722259745209192917262199844409646
15826945638023950283712168644656178523
55651641277128269186886155727162014749
34052276946595712198314943381622114006
93630743044417328478610177774383797703
72317952554341072234455125555899986461
83876764903972461167959018100035098928
64120419516355110876320426761297982652
94258829511412758412627327907988075597
51851576841264742209479721843309352972
66521001566251455299474512763155091763
67302594621329301904028379542463232585
50301096706922720227074863419005438302
65068121414213505715417505750863990767
39463351462090828889349383764393992569

48

00604067311422093312195936202982972351
16325938677224147791162957278075239505
62515816031333593823115005186268905306
58368129988108663263271980611271548858
79809348791291370749823057592909186293
91950147211975860672700925477180257503
37730799397134539532646195269996596385
65491759045833358579910201271320458390
32008538788816336376851820837278851311
75227769609787962142372162545214591281
83179821604411131167140691482717098101
54577819392023115638719508050246797257
92497605772625913328559726371211201905
72077140914864507409492671803581515757
15140503976109638467555692989703835473
14100223802583468767350129775413279532
06097115450648421218593649099791776687
47744818828706323155158650328981642282
88232746866106592732197907162384642153
48985247621678905026099804526648392954
23572873439776804957740914495383915755
65485459058976495198513801007958010783
75994577529919670054760225255203445398
87125387801719607181640781248478472579
12407824544361682345239570689514272269
75043187363326301110305342333582160933
31912188066082683414289104151732472160
53355849993224548730778822905252324234
86153152097693846104258284971496347534

49

18375620030149157032796853018686315724
88401526639835689563634657435321783493
19982554211730846774529708583950761645
82296303244243282377374505170285606980
67889521768198156710781633405266759539
42492628075696832610749532339053622309
08070814559198373553777487420290390181
42937311529334644468151212945097596534
30628421531944572711861490001765055817
70953024688752632501197052094761594167
68727784472000192789137251841622857783
79228443908430118112149636642465903363
41945406571835447719124466212593926566
20306888520055599121235363718226922531
78145879259375044144893398160865790087
61650246351970458288954817937566810464
74614105142498870252139936870509372305
44773411264135489280684105910771667782
12383328102621855877513127211793444482
01440425745083063944738363793906283008
97330624138061458941422769474793166571
76231824721683506780764875734204915576
28217583972975134478990696589532548940
33561561316740327647246921250575911625
15296545685446334981143176702572956618
44775487469378464233737238981920662048
51189437886822480727935202250179654534
37572741639107919729529508129429222053
47717304184477915673991738418311710362

52439571615271466900581470000263301045
26435478659032907332054683388720787354
44762647925297690170912007874183736735
08771337697768349634425241994995138831
50748775374338494582597655609965559543
18040920178497184685497370696212088524
37701385375768141663272241263442398215
29416453780004925072627651507890850712
65997036708726692764308377229685985169
12230503746274431085293430527307886528
39773352460174635277032059381791253969
15621063637625882937571373840754406468
96478310070458061344673127159119460843
59358259877828352665311510650416232953
29047772174083559349723758552138048305
09000964667608830154061282430874064559
44318534137552201663058121110334531207
45086824339432159043594430312431227471
38584203039010607094031523555617276799
41600203939750998976293353258555756248
08996691829864222677502360193257974726
74257821111973470940235745722227121252
68523842958742735015636600931880454933
38989741571490544182559738080871565281
43010267046028431681923039253529779576
58624143927015497408792731310516361191
37577008929564823323648298263024607975
87576774537716010249080462430185652416
17566556001608591215345562676021926899

82855377872583145144082654583484409478
46317877737479465358016996077940556870
11923286080411309046293508718271259346
68712766694873899824598527786499569165
46402945893506496433580982476596516514
20909867552038083092032304873427034682
88751604071546653834619611223013759451
57925269674364253192739003603860823645
07626988274976187235754767628899507521
14804852527950845033958570838130476937
88132112367428131948795022806632017002
24603319896719706491637411758548518784
84012054844672588851401562725019821719
06696081262778548596481836962141072171
42149863619187747545096503089570994709
34337856981674465828267911940611956037
84539785583924076127634410576675102430
75598145527861678159496570625597550743
06521085301597908073343736079432866757
89053348366955548680391343372015649883
42208933999716414797469386969054800891
93067138057171505857307148815649920714
08675825960287605645978242377024246980
53280566327870419267684671162668794634
86950464507420219373945259262668613552
94062478136120620263649819999949840514
38682852589563422643287076632993048917
23400725471764188685351372332667877921
73834754148002280339299735793615241275

52

5829569276837231234798989446274330454566790062032420516396282588443085438307
66790062032420516396282588443085438307
20149567210646053323853720314324211260
74244858450945804940818209276391400085
40422023556260218564348994145439950410
98059181794888262805206644108631900168
85681551692294862030107388971810077092
90590480749092427141018933542818429995
98816966099383696164438152887721408526
80887574882932587358099056707558170179
49161906114001908553744882726200936685
60447559655747648567400817738170330738
03054769736097865438593821872205839023
44443508867499866506040645874346005331
82743629617786251808189314436325120510
70946908135864405192295129324500788333
98788429339342435126343365204385812912
83434529730865290978330067126179813031
67943855357262969987403595704584522308
56390098913179475948752126397078375944
86113945196028675121056163897600888009
27461158608002078033415914517970730368
35196977766076373785333012024120112046
98860920933908536577322239241244905153
27809509558664594776344822699860748132
97302630975028812103517723124465095349
65369309001863776409409434983731325132
18620802148099226855029484546618147155
57444709669530177690434272031892770604

71778452793916047228153437980353967986
14243709566832214914654380145938292773
93396032754048009552231816667380357183
93275707714204672383862461780397629237
71312095807893638414479298025880655221
29262093623930637313496640186619510811
58347117331202580586672763999276357907
80638188130691563662741254312595899361
19647626101405563503399523140323113819
65623632719896183725484533370206256346
42239527669435683767613687119629218187
54576081617053031590728828700712313666
30872275491866139577373054606599743781
09876498024140112421427736680827513909
59313404155826266789510846776118665957
66016599817808941498575497628438785610
02637965431783136340251358141611519020
96499133548733131115022700681930135929
59597164019719605362503355847998096348
87180391116128135959685654788683258564
37896173159762002419621552896297904819
82219946226948713746244472909345647002
85376949588595916067892824910544125159
96300781368367490209374915732896270028
65682934443134234735123929825916673950
34259958689706972673325827359031212887
46660451461487850346142827765991608090
39865257571726308183349444182019353338
50712923457743755793440621787113300631

54

06003324053991693682603746176638565758
87758020122936635327026710068126182517
29146082025418928859352444910701382062
11553827793565296914576502048643282865
55793470720963480737269214118689546732
27677513356901901537236690368653891612
91688887876407525493494249733427181178
89275993159671935475898809792452526236
36590363200708544407845447973482918020
82044926670634420437555325050527522833
77888704080403353192340768563010934777
21256390886404131010738178533383160381
35280828119040832564401842053746792992
62203769871801806112262449090924264198
58208617511771137890516091403815750033
66424156095216328197122335023167422600
56794128140621721964184270578432895980
28823350598282081966662490358577899403
33152274817776952843681630088531769694
78369058067106482808359804669884109813
51586549069333195223943632879239905348
10987830274500172065433699066117784554
36468772363184446476806914282800455107
46866453928053994091087549391660957316
19715033166968309929466349142798780842
25722069714887558063748030886299511847
31871247772919100702275888934869394562
89515802965372150409603107761289831263
58996489341024703603664505868728758905

14068412381242473863854279082827338279
73326885504935874303160274749063129572
34974261122151741715313361862241091386
95006888358989623492763173164783400774
60886655598733382113829928776911495492
18419208777160606847287467368188616750
72210172611038306717878566948129487850
48943063086169948798703160515884108282
35127415353851336589533294862949449506
18685147791058046960390693726626703865
12905201137810586161888869479576074 13
58553458515176805197333443349523012039
57707396237713160302428872005373209982
53008977618973129817881944671731160647
23147624845755192873278282512718244680
78242152164695678192940982389262849437
60248852279003620219386696482215628093
60537317804086372726842669642192994681
92149087017075333610947913818040632873
87593848269535583077395761447997270003
47288018278528138950321798634521611106
66088393140532269449054555278678944175
79202440021450780192099804461382547805
85804844241640477503153605490659143007
81583724301231375115622840158386442708
90718284816757527123846782459534334449
62201009607105137060846180118754312072
54913349942476171156333214089346091565
61550600317384218701570226103101916603

88706466143889773631878094071152752817
46895764015810470169652475577408916445
68677717158500583269943401677202156767
72406812836656526412298243946513319735
91997094032759385026695574702318132032
43716420586141033606524536939160050644
95306016126782264894243739716671766123
10489750318857321655549883421218028469
12529086101485527815277625623750456375
76949773433684601560772703550962904939
24870884062810679436224187047470083688
42671022558302403599841645951122485272
63363264511401739524808619463584078375
35568856223171155209472230654370926067
97351000565549381224575483728545711797
39361575616764169289580525729752233855
86113883221711073622658162188424431788
57488798109026653793426664216990914056
53643224930133486798815488662866505234
69972355747384248305904236771432787923
16422403877764330192600192284778313837
63253612102533693581262408686669973827
59773656822279072158324788886423693463
96164363308730139814211430306008730666
16480367898409133592629340230432497492
68878316436026810113095707161419128306
86577323532639653677390317661361315965
55358499939860056515592193675997771793
30197446881483711032065036931928945214

02650915465184309936553493337183425298
43367991593941746622390038952767381333
06177476295749438687169784537672194935
06590875711917720875477107189937960894
77451265475750187119487073873678589020
06173733210756933022163206284320656711
92096950585761173961632326217708945426
21460985841023781321581772760222273813
34954104810030732751077999489919779638
83530734443457532975914263768405442264
78421606312276964696715647399904371590
33239065607266441164386054048388471619
12109008701019130726071044114143241976
79682854788552477947648180295973604943
97004795960402927462992035720997619501
40348315380947714601056333446998820822
12058728151072918297121191787642488035
46723169165418522567292344291871281632
32596965413548589577133208339911288775
91722611527337901034136208561457799239
87783250835507301998184590259583559892
60553299673770491722454935329683300002
23018151722657578752405883224908582128
00897479093261007625787704286560069961
76212176845478996440705066241710213327
48679623743022915535820078014116534806
56474882306150033920689837947662550365
49822805329662862117930628430170492402
30198571997894883689718304380518217441

58

91476604297524372516834354112170386313
79411422095295885798060152938752753799
03093887168357209576071522190027937929
27863036372687658226812419933848081660
21603722154710143007377537792699069587
12128928801905203160128586182549441335
38207848834653116326504076424283908701
21015194231961652268422003711230464300
67344206474771802135307012409886035339
91526679238711017062218658835737812109
35179775604425634694999787251125440854
52227481091487430725986960204027594117
89425812818821599523596589791811440776
53354321757595255536158128001163846720
31934650729680799079396371496177431211
94020212975731251652537680173591015573
38153772001952444543620071848475663415
40744232862106099761324348754884743453
96659813387174660930205350702719529839
43271425371155766600025784423031073429
55153394506048622276496668762407932435
31929926392537310768921353525723210808
89819339168668278948281170472624501948
40970097576092098372409007471797334078
81418251958425980962417476101382526439
55135259311885045636264188300338539652
43599741693132289471987830842760040136
80747039040972384739458348961865397905
94118599310356168436869219485382055780

59

39577388136067954990008512325944252972
44866667668346414021899159445653094234
40650667851948417766779470472041958822
04329538032631053749488312218039127967
84461001397267538921951191178365876625
28083690053249004597410947068772912328
21430463533728351995364827432583311914
44590178096077828835837301118575436599
58982724531925310588115026307542571493
94302445393187017992360816661130542625
39958338979429716020703387678150330102
80120095997252222280801423571094760351
92554443492998676781789104555906301595
38097618759203589373419789623589311259
83902598310267193304189215109689156225
06965911982832345550305908173073519550
37216658702880539921385760370353771051
78021280129566841984140362872725623214
42875430221090947272107347413497551419
07370433182766261772759968888260272252
47133683353452816692779591328861381766
34985772893690096574956228710302436259
07724122190943008717556926257580657099
12016659622436080242870024547362036394
84125595488172727247365346778364720191
83039987176270375157246499222894679323
22693619177641614618795613956699567783
06829031658969943076733350823499079062
41002025061340573443006957454746821756

90441651540636584680463692621274211075
39904218871612761778701425886482577522
38891845995233762923779155857445494773
61295525952226578636462118377598473700
34797140820699414558071908021359073226
92331008317595106590191212947954086036
40757358750205890208704579670007055262
50581142066390745921527330940682364944
15908910092202966805233252661989113118
42016291631076894084723564366808182168
65721968826835840278550078280404345371
01836510969517823357430305048526537380
73531074185917705610397395062640355442
27515610110726177937063472380499066692
21619711942591204450846417463835899382
39946517395509000859479990136026674261
49429006646711506717542217703877450767
35637421547829059110126191575558702389
57001405117822646989944917908301795475
87676016809410013583761357859135692445
56477644641786671153919513576961048649
22490083446715486383054477914330097680
48687834818467273375843689272431044740
68076852786255851650920882638132336231
48733336714764520450876627614950389949
50480956046098960432912335834885999029
45264002849942808786240398118148847673
01216754161106629995553668193123287425
70206373835202008686369131173346973174

```
12191536332467453256308713473027921749
56227014687325867891734558379964351358
80095935087755635624881049385299900767
51355135277924124292774885658885665132
47302514710210575352516511814850902750
47684551825209633189906852761443513821
36621523688905787866994322888160283774
82035506016029894009119713850179871683
63374413927597364401700701476370665570
35043381211135764150184518214136198234
95159601064752712575935185304332875537
78305750956742544268471221961870917856
07839361445113833356491032564057338986
67178123972237519316430617013859539474
36784339267098671245221118969084023632
74114966012434830989299417380305884171
66613073040067588380432111555379440605
49772170594282151488616567277124090338
77277456290971101348851843741186956554
49745736845218066982911045058004299887
95389902780438359628240942186055628778
84288021275538848037286400194416142574
99904272009595204654170598104989967504
51193647117277222043610261407975080968
69751766002371877483480161203102346805
67112644766123747627852190241202569943
53471622666089367521983311181351114650
38548950251206557726361454736044268594
98074396932331297127377157347099713952
```

62

29118265348515558713733662912024271430
25037632695013509116129529937858646813
07226486008270881333538193703682598867
89332123832705329762585738279009782646
05455985551318366888446282651337984916
67839409761353766251798258249663458771
95012438404035914084920973375464247448
81761840700235695801774101776969250778
14893386672557898564589851056891960924
39884156928069698335224022563457049731
22452693541938370048431833571965166267
21575524193401933099018319309196582920
96965624766768365964701959575473934551
43374137087615173236772042273856742791
70698204549953095918872434939524094441
67899884631984550485239366297207977745
28143994182567894577957125524268260899
40863317371538896262889629402112108884
42737656862452761213037101730078513571
54045330415079594477761435974378037424
36646973247138410492124314138903579092
41603640631403814983148190525172093710
39640268089948325722979545640427017577
22904173234796073618787889913318305843
06939482596131871381642346721873084513
38772190869751049428437693250249816566
73816260615941768252509993741672883951
74406693254965340310145222531618900923
53764863784828813442098700480962271712

26407489571939002918573307460104360729
19094576799461492929042798168772942648
77299528584346477753869069501489841339
24540394144680263625402118614317031251
11757764282991464453340892097696169909
83726523617687456058947049681701369749
09523072082682887890730190018253425805
34342170592871393173799314241085264739
09482845964180936141384758311361305761
08462366837237695913492615824516221552
13487924414504175684806412063652017038
63301295327776990231186480200675569056
82295016354931992305914246396217025329
74757311409422018019936803502649563695
58664259067626856873721103391567938398
95765565193177883000241613539562437777
84080174881937309502069990089089932808
83974303677365955248913001566332940779
07139615464534088791510300651321934486
67324827590794680787981942501958262232
03951312520141099605312606965554042486
70549986786923021746989009547850725672
97879476988883109348746442640071818316
03316555115342761556224054744733780492
46214952133258527698847336269182649174
33898782478927846891882805466998230368
99397834137475870258057163494135684339
29396068192061773317917382085624364336
63535986349449689078106401967407443658

36670715869245211829978938040771375012
90858646578905771426833582768978554717
68718442772612050926648610205153564284
06323684818072879407171279668200607275
59555904040233178749447346454760628189
54151213916291844429765106694796935401
68660100551960776873353965116149309375
70968554559381513789569039251014953265
62814701199832699220006639287537471313
52364215892651262040728877165783584052
19646054105435443642166562244565042999
01025658692727914275293117208279393775
13261060528812353734510683729398935808
71243869385934389175713376300720319760
81660446468393772580690923729752348670
29169104263692620901996052041210240776
48190316014085863558427609537086558164
27399534934654631450404019952853725200
49578052546562511541092524379913262627
13609099402902262062836752132305065183
93405745011209934146491843332364656937
17259144893241590062420206128857329261
33596808726500045628284557574596592120
53034131011182750130696150983551563200
43107846019065654938065425252291619918
19959602752327702249855738824899882707
46593635576858256051806896428537685077
20122203479209939361792682065901421656
15925306737944568949070853263568196831

65

86177226824991147261573203580764629811
62440133167378927886892290325933498617
97021994981925739617673075834417098559
22217017182571277753449150820527843090
46194608352174020058386728497094110232
66953921445461066215006410674740207009
18991195137646690448126725369153716229
07913854039375600778351533741677479421
00384002308951850994548779039346122220
86506016050035177626483161115332558770
50735412792499098593734737870811942530
55121436979749914951860535920403830235
71635272763087469321962219006426088618
36761033460022554774778136410126919065
69686495012688376296907233961276287223
04114181361006026404403003599698891994
58273976241146137448040596970625767647
23766065541618574690527229238228275186
79915698339074767114610302277660602006
12468764777288190967916133540198814027
57992174167678799231603963569492851513
63364721954061117176738737255572852294
00543617851765023075446938693078734991
10352182532929726044553210797887711449
89887091151123725060423875373484125708
60640690520584521227545338480082053024
50456517669518576913200042816758054924
81178051983264603244579282973012910531
83856368212062155312886685649565126138

92261367064093953334570526986959692350
35309422454386527867767302754040270224
63844835532399147513634410440500923303
61271496081355490531539021002299595756
58370538126196568314428605795669662215
47216956208700137277685369608407048333
25132793112232507148630206951245395003
73572334680709465648308920980153487870
56334910923660575540508641115214414814
34630437273271045027768661953107858323
33485784029716092521532609255893265560
06721243594642550659967717703884453961
81632879614460817789272171836908880126
77820743010642252463480745430047649288
55534090621851536543554741254761527697
72667769772777058315801412185688011705
02836527554321480348800444297999806215
79045641619572127845089284898064264974
27090579129069217807298769477975112447
30599140605062994689428093103421641662
99356148281309988707452927160484336308
18404126469637925843094185442216359084
57614607855856247381493142707826621518
55416038702068769804617474008083243436
65382354555109449498431093494759944672
67366535251766270677219418319197719637
80157021699336750837600571634546436717
76723387588643405644871566964321041282
59564534984138841289042068204700761559

67

6916843038999348366793542549210328113
6318472259230555438305820694167562999 2
0133731754891220372303490726810685344 5
4035993561823576312837767640631013125 3
3521214199461186935083317658785204711 2
3643312267651299641713252175135532618 6
7681942338790365468908001827135283584 8
8844411176123410117991870923650718485 7
8562210211040097769944531217950224795 7
8069506532965940383987369907240797679 0
4082679400761872954783596349279390457 6
9736616434053597922192858705749574816 9
6694062334272619733518136626063735982 5
7555249650980726012366828360592834185 5
8480269584137725589708837899429105498 0
0331113884603401939166122186696058491 5
7148573356828614950001909759112521880 0
3964197621635593757437180114805594422 9
8730418196808085647265713547612831629 2
0044988031540210553059707666636274932 8
3089168809323592900817874119857383171 9
2616728834918402429721290434965526942 7
2640255964146352591434840067586769035 0
3823205729341329815935330444464968294 4
1367323442158380761694831219333119819 0
6109614295220153617029857510559432646 1
4685054526849757648078080092213358113 7
8197749271768545075538328768874474591 5
9373116247060109124460982942484128752 0

68

224462594477638749491997840446829257360
968534549843266536862844489365704111817
793806441616531223600214918768769467398
407517176307516849856359201486892943105
940202457969622924566644881967576294349
535326382171613395757790766370764569570
259738800438415805894336137106551859987
600754924187211714889295221737721146081
154344982665479872580056674724051122007
383459271575727715218589946948117940644
466399432370044291140747218180224825837
736017346685300744985564715420036123593
397312914458591522887408719508708632218
837288262822884631843717261903305777147
651564143822306791847386039147683108141
358275585364359772165002827780371342286
968878734979509603110889919614338666406
845069742078770028050936720338723262963
785603865321643234881555755701846908907
464787912243637555666867806761054495501
726079114293083128576125448194444947324
481909379536900820638463167822506480953
181040657025432760438570350592281891987
806586541218429921727372095510324225107
971807783304260908679427342895573555925
272380551144043800123904168771644518022
649168164192740110645162243110170005669
112173318942340054795968466980429801736
25704067

33282129962153684881404102194463424646
22074557564396045298531307140908460849
96537678037932018991408658146621753193
37665970114330608625009829566917638846
05676297293146491149370462446935198403
95344491351411936679330193661766365325
55149174982307987072280860859626112660
50428929696653565251668888557211227680
27727437089173896397722575648905334010
38855931125679991516589025016486961427
20700591605616615970245198905183296927
89355503039346812197615821839804839605
62523091462638447386296039848924386187
29850777592879272206855480721049781765
32862101874767668972488411395603494803
76727036316921007350834073865261684507
48249644859742813493648037242611670426
68708319250409976153190768557703274217
85010006441984124207396400139603601583
81056592841368457411910273642027416372
34882145241013477165296031284086584197
87951116511529827814620379139855006399
96032659124852530849369031313010079997
71913622308660110999291428712493885416
12038020411340188887219693477904497527
45428807280350930582875442075513481666
09278793535665212556201399882496284787
26214432362853676502591450468377635282
58765213915648097214192967554938437558

70

26002531685363567313792624758780494459
44183429172756988376226261846365452743
49766241113845130548144983631178978448
97320767195087841586188796929558197332
50699951402601511675529750575437810242
23895792578656212843273120220071673057
40692868693639301867659582513264991459
50260917069347519408975357464016830811
79884645247361895605647942635807056256
32811892696630264795359510971276591362
33180866921535788607812759910537171402
20450618607537486630635059148391646765
67232057145168861707909846959322367249
46737583099607042589220481550799132752
08858378111768521426933478692189524062
26579210436203488529262679840139532164
58791151579050460579710838983371864038
02441751134722647254701079479399695355
46696197267632552299146549334996632341
85951450360980344092212206712567698723
42794070885707047429317332918852389672
19713539244924261786411886377909628144
86917869468177591717150669111480020759
43201206196963779510322708902956608556
22254526026104607361313688690092817210
68198618553780982018471154163630326265
69928342415502360097804641710852553761
27289053350455061356841437758544296779
77014660294387687225115363801191758154

71

0281208182556064854107879335989210644 2
7244898618961629413418001295130683638 6
0929410008313667337215300835269623573 7
1753307386533382048421903081864491840 9
3723944033405244909554558016406460761 5
8101030176748847501766190869294609876 9
2016912021816882910408707095609514704 1
6921147027413390052253340834812870353 0
3102391969997859741390859360543359969 7
0756044601342424536824960987725813110 2
4732798562072126572499003468293886872 3
0489556225320446360263985422525841646 4
3242716114198178024825955635449072192 2
6583863662663750835944314877635156145 7
1074552801615967704844271419443518327 5
6984075526779264112617652506159652354 5
7187956673170913319358761628255920783 0
8018520689015150471334038610031005591 4
8178521103847545429333891884441205179 4
3969970194112695119526564919594189975 4
1839323464742429070271887522353439367 3
6336632003072327470374071239825620246 6
2651974090199762452056198557625760008 7
0817308328834438183107005451449354588 5
4226785785519153722923795554943334101 7
4420169600090696415612732297770221217 9
5186837635908225512881647002199234886 4
0439591530184640047143211863606225270 1
1541122283802778538911098490201342741 0

72

14121559769965438877197485376431158229
83853312307175113296190455900793806427
66958190148426279912217929479873489018
68471676503827328552059082984529806259
25035212845192592798659350613296194679
62523739725655841578537445675589980324
05492186962888490332560851455344391660
22625777551291620077279685262938793753
04541810807292858919897153817973434961
87232927614747850192611450413274873242
97058340847111233374627461727462658241
53242710593225062553023147387592517247
87322881491455915605036334575424233779
16037495250249302235148196138116256391
14156103268449580725082734317659440540
98269765269344579863479709743124498271
93311386387315963636121862349726140955
60799206283169994200720548115253533939
46076850019909886553861433495781650089
96164907967814290114838764568217491407
56237676184537751440314754112067601607
26460556859257799322070337333398916369
50434669069482843662998003741452762771
65476238255461708831898108688068478537
05536480469350958818025360529740793538
67651119507937328208314626896007107517
55206144337841145499501364324463281933
46389050936545714506900864483440180428
36339051357815727397333453728426337217

4065775771079830517555721036795976901889958494130195999573017901240193908681
3565855396619413717944876320798688003716073032205474235722668968018821234243
9188598416897227765219403249322731479366923400484897605903795809469604175427
9613782553781223947646147832926976545162290281701100437846038756544151739433
9600489153188175766505009516974024156447712936566142539493688842305174001299
2055685428985389794266995677702708914651373689220610441548166215680421983847
6730871787590279209175900695273456682026513373111518000181434120962601658629
8210766635233617740078377834237091526440630540718078433580610729611055500204
1513169637304684921335683726540030750982908936461204789111475303704989395283
3457824082817386441322710002968311940203323456420826473276233830294639378998
3758365545599193408662350909679611340048670271231765266637107787251118603540
3755448741869351973365662177235922939677646325156202348757011379571209623772
3431370212031004965152111976013176419408203437348512852602913334915125083119
8028501778557107253731491392157091051309650598859999315608636554774035518981
6673353588004821466509974143376118277

72335191074121757284159258087259131507
46060256349037772633739144613770380213
18347447301113032670296917335047701632
10661622783002726928336558401179141944
78087482533607144032962522857750098085
99609040936312635621328162071453406104
22411208301000858726425211226248014264
75194261843258533867538740547434910727
10049754281159466017136122590440158991
60022982780179603519408004651353475269
87776095278399843680869089891978396935
32179980139135442552717910225397010810
63214304851137829149851138196914304349
75001899806816444121232733283071928243
62406733196554692677851193152775113446
46890550424811336143498460484905125834
56832664415284897139723760403282126602
53516693914082049947320486021627759791
77123475109750240307893575993771509502
17516935558270725339118923340702238320
77585802137174778378778391015234132098
48942345961369234049799827930414446316
27072147961174569757196812392919137409
82925805561955207434243295982898980529
23336641541925636738068949420147124134
05250722040617943552525552250087487900
86568314542835167750542294803274783044
05643858159195266675828292970522612762
87110401348017872248017896840524079243

75

6058274246744307672164527031345135416764966890127478680101029513386269864974821211862904033769156857624069929637249309720162870720018983542369036414927023696193854737248032985504511208919287982987446786412915941753167560253343531062674525450711418148323988060729714023472552071349079839898235526872395090936566787899238371257897624875599044322889538837731734894112275707141095979004791930104674075041143538178246463079598955563899188477378134134707024674736211204898622699188851745625173251934135203811586335012391305444191007362844756751416105041097350585276204448919097890198431548528053398577784431393388399431044446566924455088594631408175122033139068159659251054685801313383815217641821043342978882611963044311138879625874609022613090084997543039577124323061690626291940392143974027089477766370248815549932245882597902063125743691094639325280624164247686849545532493801763937161563684785982371590238542126584061536722860713170267474013114526106376538339031592194346981760535838031061288785205154693363924108846763200956708971836749057816308515813816196688222204757043759061433804072585386208356517

6998426774523195824182683698270160 2374
1493836349662935157685406139734274 6470
8996856181701605511048809715548591 1861
7189668025973541705423985135560018 7203
3507906094642127114399319604652742 4050
8822253597734815191354385712532585 4049
3946010865793798058620143366078825 2197
1780902581737087091646045272797715 3509
9103407364250203863867182205228796 9445
8387652947951048660717390229327455 4267
8566977686593992341683412227466301 5062
1553205026553414609952493560508549 2175
6549134830958906536175693817637473 6441
8337897422970070354520666317092960 7591
9896277324230902523974438610142630 9868
7733913882518684316501027964911497 7375
8288891345034114886594867021549210 1084
3280807834280894172980089832975369 4064
4969903125399863919581601468995220 8806
6228540841486427478628197554662927 8814
6216071713818801808405720847158689 0683
6919393381864278454537956719272397 9723
6465166759201105799566396259853551 2763
5587681402134098290162968734298507 9247
1846056874828331381259161962476156 9028
7590107273310329914062386460833337 8638
2579263023915900035576090324772813 3888
7339178096966014696150317542267511 259
9331552967421333630022296490648093 4582

77

00818106180210022766458040027821333675
85730190113717546727630590443531313190
36092489097246427928455549913490005180
29570708291905255678188991389962513866
23193800536113462242946102489540724048
57123256628888931722116432947816190554
86805494344103409068071608802822795968
69501336438142682521704728708630101373
01155236861416908375675747637239763185
75703810944339056456446852418302814810
79983769185121272019350440418046047216
26939445788377090105974693219720558114
07877598977207200968938224930323683051
58626572811146379969831375179376232151
11252349734305240622105244234353732905
65516340666950616589287821870775679417
60807129737813351871179316500331555238
22487730653444179453415395202424449703
41012087407218810938826816751204229940
49481794494727328947701115741394412284
55521828424922240658752689172272780607
11675404697300803703961878779669488255
56146743843925701158295466613586786718
97661297311267200072971553613027503556
16781776544228744211472988161480270524
38068176535732755786025058470840132088
37932816008769081300492491473682517035
38221961903901499952349538710599735114
34782923394991879366086923013755963685

78

32373806703591144243268561512109404259
58263930167801712866923928323105765885
17140202111969570647998140315056330451
41564414623163763809904402816256917576
48914256971416359843931743327023781233
69380430128926263753826677950341693343
23607500248175741808750388475094939454
89620974048544263563716499594992098088
42947903636662975260032438563529458447
28944547166209297495496616877414120882
13047702281611645604400723635158114972
97392189667373826472047226422212420165
60150284971306332795814302516013694825
56701478093579088965713492615816134690
18069650895563101212184918058479227206
91871696316330044858020102860657858591
26997463766174146393415956953955420331
46280265189511679380745733157598460861
73702687867602943677780500244673391332
43166988035407323238828184750105164133
11895370364884226902704780527424906034
92082954755054003457160184072574536938
14553117535421072655783561549987444748
04273234578800618731493415660463529797
79455075359304795687209316724536547208
38168585560604380197703076424608348987
61013457093948770029461757920619525492
55757109038525171488525265671045349813
41980339064152987634369542025608027761

79

44219143189213939088345431317696851018
40103844472348948869520981943531906506
55535461733581404554483788475252625394
96658699920584176527801253410338964698
18642430034146791380619028059607854888
01078970551694621522877309010446746249
79799926271209516847795684825833414022
66477210843362437593741610536734041954
73896419789542533503630186140095153476
69614762556518738232924685473569358028
96011536791787303553159378363082248615
17777054157757656175935851201669294311
11388635821596676188303261041646517148
46979385422621687161400122378213779774
13126897726671299202592201740877007695
62834739322010881593562862819285635718
93384958850603853158179760679479840878
36097596014973342057270460352179060564
76032855692762734951822032361441125841
82426247712012035776388895974318232827
87131460805353357449429762179678903456
81698895535185044783256163807094769516
99086247100019748809205009521943632378
71976487033922381154036347548862684595
61597551937654101150140670012269274743
93888589943859730245414801061235908036
27458528849356325158538438324249325266
60875889083187007091002373771065769850
56433928854337658342596750653715005333

51448990829388773735205145933304962653
14151413861244379358850709446880454869
75358170212908490787347806814366323322
81941582734567135644317153796781805819
58524648400840329099819437817181773023
17003989733050495387356116261023999433
25978012689343260558471027876490107092
34438846340117355568659035852449193701
81041626208504299258697435817098133894
04593447193749387762423240985283276226
66049423851297094532455862521036008292
86649724174919141988966129558076770979
59479530601311915901177394310420904907
94244488685130868444937059090260061206
49425744710353547657859242708130410618
54621988183009063458818703875585627491
15873754210646679513464875867715438380
18521348281915812462599335160198935595
16796893285220582479942103451271587716
33452229954188396804488355297533612868
37225935390079201666941339091168758803
98882886921600237325736158820716351627
13328105181876021048521806755266486739
08900907195138058626735124312215691637
90227732870541084203784152568328871804
69879525130732663402785190594173389203
58540395677035611329354482585628287610
61069822972142096199350933131217118789
10787668720445488760894101747986471378

81

8246215395593333275562009439580434537
9197822805903959599274369137937786649 4
0964048777841748336432684026282932406 2
6008190808180439091455635193685606304 5
0891422896452199877988493474777291327 9
7266027658401667890136490508741142126 8
6196986204412696528298108704547986155 9
5453380212011556469799767857389201862 4
3599326777689454060508218838227909833 6
2716712449002676117849826437703300208 1
8445900097172352043319947082420987715 1
4449751017055643029542821819670009202 5
1561584417420593365814813490269311151 7
0938722600264586305613256057925609273 3
2265579346280805683443921373688405650 4
3430739657406101777937014142461549307 0
7413608054421002956000956635889778992 6
7630517718781943706761498217564186590 1
1616086540863539151303920131680576903 4
1725964536923508064174465623515239290 5
0409479953184074862151210561833854566 1
7665260639371365880252166622357613220 1
9417013726649660732520107719479312652 8
2763302413805164907174565964853748354 6
6919452358031530196916048099460681490 4
0378198297323609300871357607986214254 2
2096419004367905479049930078372421581 9
5453541837112936865843055384271762803 5
2791288211293083515756565999447417884 3

82

83815651484342298587042455924346932952
32821803508333726283791830216591836181
55421715744846577842013432998259456688
45582661719790121808494803324487872581
83774805522268151011371745368417870280
27445244290547451823467491956418855124
44213377835214238659799259882032870851
09338386829906571994614906290257427686
03885051103263854454041918495886653854
50405713236296810691468148478696591668
61842756798460041868762298055562963045
95322792305161672159196867584952363529
89357885077460815373214546429847923105
11676357749494622952569497660359473962
43099534331040499420967788382700271447
84940690370732491064441516960532565605
86778757417472110827435774315194060757
98356362914332639781221894628744779811
98072256467146640548501310096567863148
80090303749338875364183165134982546694
67331611812336485439764932502617954935
72043054021829748712511074040116114058
99911093062492312813116340549262571356
72181862893278613883371802853505650359
19527414008695109261675414767926680321
09237467087213606278332922386413619594
12133927803611827632410600474097111104
81400036233427145144833346416754663546
99731494756643423659493496845884551524

83

15075637660508663282742479413606287604
12906449138285194564026431532258586240
43141838669590633245063000392213192647
62596269151090445769530144405461803785
75030366862124622786397527466678701210
03392984873375014475600322100622358029
34377495503203701273846816306102657030
08722754629667968808905871276763610662
25722352229739206443093524327228100859
97309513252863060110549791564479184500
46180467624089289256809129305929606423
57021061524646205023248966593987324933
96737695202399176089847457184353193664
65291258480644801965201628387951894993
36759241485626136995945307287254532463
29152911012876377060557060953137752775
18679232921349552451330898679691651290
73841302167573238637575820080363575728
00275449032795307990079944254110872569
31880146679355958346764328688769666100
97395749967836593397846346959948950610
49038364740950469522606385804675807306
99122904740898791668721171475276447116
04401952718169508289733537148530928937
04638442089329977112585684084660833993
40456890267875160087754612679880154658
56522061210953490796707365539702576199
43137663996060606110640695933082817187
64260435734253617569437848484952501082

84

6648839515970049059838081210521111091
9433239511360514464598342107990580820
3716464523127704023160072138543723461
6726099787038565709199850759563461324
4601884098501942876879022687345565005
9121546544063829253851276317663922050
3834520430077301702994036261543400132
7639109129883278639204123004455516840
4889809080779174636092439334912641164
4009388074635660726233669584276458369
2687348158819610585718357674620096505
6065929263548291499045768307210893245
5707370166071739819448502884260396366
7460311847862258310565808708703055675
5861341700745402965687634774176431051
5103673286924555858208237203860178173
4051751304379948688223200443780431031
0921034261674998000073016094814586374
8877852227307633049538394434538277060
7607635420984450083062476302535727810
2783461766970544287155315340016497076
5719598504174819908720149087568603778
5919947193433527729472855379257876848
2301101859365800717291186967617655053
7503029303383070644891281141202550615
8964110076238245744886551825810581403
5320124754723269087547507078577659732
4284445935304499207001453874894822655
4422236963655441942254413382122254774

75354946248276805333369832841561386923
63443358553868471111430498248398991803
16545863828935379913053522283343013795
33729540162576232280811384994918761441
41322933767106563492528814528239506209
02235787668465011666009738275366040544
69416534222390521083145858470355293522
19928272760574821266065291385530345549
74455147034493948686342945965843102419
07859236802245607639367841662705185551
78702904073557304620639692453307795782
24594971042018804300018388142900817303
94505073427870131244668600927785818110
40911511729374873627887874907465285565
43474888683106411005102302087510776891
87815256227352515503795324448577872776
17001964853703555167655209119339343762
86628461984402629525218367852236747510
88097815070989784130862458815226609635
51401874495836926917799047120726494905
73726428600521140358123107600669951853
61248627467563758962252991164960668765
08261734178484789337295056739007878617
92535144062104536625064046372881569823
23175005962610809219552111508593029556
54967538862612972339914628358476048627
62702730973920200143224870758233735491
52460856082103288297418390647886992 32
73691360048837436615223517058437705545

21081551336126214291181561530175888257
35948925071088792621286413924433093837
97333867806131795237315266773820858024
70143352700924380326695174211950767088
43263464427491275589077468635821621660
42741315170212458586056233631493164646
91394656249747174195835421860774871105
73384584336899396459137406033821593522
43594751626239188685307822821763983237
30618020424656047752794310479618972429
95330297924974816840528937910449470045
90864991872727345413508101983881864673
60939257193051196864560185578245021823
10658894379865224320506773799661969554
72440585922417953006820451795370043472
45176289356677050849021310773662575169
73355274623029430312035962609534235743
97249659211010657817826108745318874803
18743082357369919515634095716270099244
49297491054898515196586647401482251063
35367949737142510229341882585117371994
49911509758374613010550506419772153192
93548753711916302620303285886585284801
93509225875775597425276584011721342323
64808402714335636754204637518255252494
43296570438613878659019657388028684018
94087672816714137033661732650120578653
91578070308871426151907500149257611292
76751930967284539711602136063030905422

4396632067432358279788933232440577919
9278484633339777737655901870574806828
6783479656241461028995084873996929707
5043275302997287229732793444298864641
2725348160603779707298299173029296308
6958019963124133049393504933254123550
71054461182591141116454534710329881047
8440677801380771314654000993863064812
6661433085820681139583831916954555825
9426895769841428893743467084107946318
9325391069639557807060212459748982935
6461356078898347241997947856436204209
4613412387613198865352358312996862268
9486084084566556068769545012744866314
0505473535174687300980632278046891224
6821460806727627708402402266155485024
00895289165711761743902033758487784291
12896232470591918746910420058483261406
7733375102719565399469716251724831223
0633919328707983800748485726516123434
9332733566644733585564302352808839243
4827876088616494328939916639921048830
7847777048045728491456303353265070029
5889062659154985094079727675671297950
1009822947622896189159144152003228387
8773485130790810191292672271037788980
5396415636236416915498576840839846886
1684375407065121039062506128107663799
0479088796747780697384731704752534421
5639038720123880632368803

70179493089549007763315230635483742568
16653361606641980030188287123767481898
33024683637148830925928337590227894258
80600872860388591688497306939480205112
21766359138251524278670094406942355120
20156837777885182467002565170850924962
37477268136942843500629388144299879053
01056217375459182679973217735029368928
06521002539626880749809264345801165571
58867004435039765053234782873273688408
63540002740676783821963522226539290939
80736739136408289872201777674716811819
58561337215831190546829360832369761134
50281757830202934845982925000895682630
27126329586629214765314223335179309338
79513570953463771836840924444220963193
31295620305575517340067973740614162107
92363342380564685009203716715264255637
18538895714164197723874226105966673969
97173168169415435095283193556417705668
62221521799115135563970714331289365755
38446483262012064243380169558626985610
22460646069330793847858814367407000599
76970364901927332882613532936311240365
06986521606389872502672380874033967443
97830258296894256896741864336134979475
24552629142652284241924308338810358005
37870239995421721136865502753413622116
93140694669513186928102574795985605145

00502171591331775160995786555198188619
32112821107094422872404424811534060558
95958355815232012184605820563592699303
47885113206862662758877144603599665610
84307256965005630644891875994665967728
47171539573612108180841547273142661748
93313417463266235422207260014601270120
69346395205644455432916629866607830890
68118790090815295063626782075614388815
78135113469536630387841209234694286873
08393204323338727754968052103028215443
24723388845215343727250128589747691460
80831440412586818154004918777228786980
18534545370065266556491709154295227567
09222217474112062720656622989806032891
67206874365494824610869736722554740481
28892424718543236057534116728507575520
57131156697954584887398742228135887985
84078313506054829055148278529489112190
53831956242287194847594078593980479010
94194070671764439032730712135887385049
99363883820550168340277749607027684488
02819122206368886368110435695293006521
95528261526991271637277388418993287130
56346468822739828876319864570983630891
77864870866761854856800476725526754147
42851028145807403152992197814557756843
68111018531749816701642664788409026268
28244482580275320945499151045185177165

46311804904567985713257528117913656278
15811128881656228587603087597496384943
52756766121689592614850307853620452745
07752950631012480341804584059432926079
85443562009370809182152392037179067812
19922804960697382387433126267303067959
43960954957189577217915597300588693646
84557667609245090608820221223571925453
67151918348725874239194108904441159599
32760044506556206461164655665487594247
36925233695599303035509581762617623184
95619064948396730020377638743693439998
29430209147073618947932692762445186560
23955905370512897816345542332011497599
48962784243274837880327014186769526211
80975006405149755889650293004867605208
01049153788541390942453169171998762894
12772211294645682948602814931815602496
77887949813777216229359437811004448060
79767242927624951078415344642915084276
45200020427694706980417758322090970202
91657347251582904630910359037842977572
65172087724474095226716630600546971638
79431711968734846887381866567512792985
75016363411314627530499019135646823804
32997069577015078933772865803571279091
3767420805655493624646

Notes

The 100000 decimal points of pi presented in this book are intended to be accurate. Whilst the author offers no guarantees as to the accuracy of the information presented in this book, the author believes that it is an accurate work.

This work presents merely 100000 digits of pi. "Merely", because computer algorithms have reached beyond ten trillion digits (10000000000050 is the world record at the time of going to print).

Nobody, however, has been verified to have memorised more than 100000 digits by Guinness World Records (at the time of going to print). This book hopefully gives you a good idea of what you'd have to memorise to beat that record.

Mathematical methodology is believed to be the only way to remember that many digits. Traditional memory techniques such as remembering a story or poem linked to the thing you are trying to remember are said to be ineffectual for remembering this many digits.

Something really rather special would be required to remember 10 trillion digits.

Pi comes with quite a lot of repeating digits – you can find quite a few repetitions of 5 digits in this book, for example. Can you find 999999 in this book? (p_____, for future reference).

Did you know...

...that pi was called the Ludolphian number in Germany until around 100 years ago, due to the approximations of pi made by Ludolph van Ceulen from 1596 onwards?

...that a circle with a radius of 1 has an area of π?

...that a sphere with a diameter of 1 has an area of π?

...that pi has only been known as the Greek letter π since the mid-18th Century?

...that pi is sometimes known as "Archimedes's Constant" because his polygonal method of calculation for pi was dominant for over a millennium?

...that the Greek letter π used to represent pi is a minuscule (lowercase) character?

...that a Persian astronomer, called Jamshīd al-Kāshī, held the world record for digits of pi, by calculating 16 digits, for over 140 years?

...that the Great Pyramid's construction is believed (controversially) by some experts to show knowledge of the concept of pi?

...that the world record of ten trillion and fifty digits of pi took 371 days to calculate, and 45 hours to verify?

...that March 13th is National Pi Day in the US (because they write the date as 3/14)?

...that National Pie Day in the US is celebrated on January 23rd – well, you can't have everything, can you?